the good the bad & the ugly

a short collection of poems by
kayla kim

the good the bad & the ugly

she told me to write
whenever it hurt
so i got down on my knees
and scrambled for words in the darkness

-and that's how it started

the good the bad & the ugly

contents

the good..4

the bad……………………………………………………………………………..25

the ugly……………………………………………………………………………..36

the good

the good the bad & the ugly

you are loved you are loved you are loved

-gentle reminder

the good the bad & the ugly

i woke up and caught the end of a
really nice sunrise and
had a really swell cup of tea and
i could feel it
the healing
so today i will scream out the window
it won't always be easy
i will not always be able to get out of bed
but today i did

-it's brave to wake up and do what you can

the good the bad & the ugly

and i think maybe
just maybe
you were put on this earth
for your heart to stop
and then start again
just to remind us
that it's possible

i hope to learn how to
suffer with half the
grace
kindness
warmth
humility and
strength
that you do

-to hana

the good the bad & the ugly

you tell me what i do doesn't matter
because really
at the end of the day
how much can one human do
but really
love is a funny little thing
that one human can do

the good the bad & the ugly

i tried to count how many people's lives
you've made better
but lost count somewhere
in the thousands
what you have said and done
has shaped strangers
what you say and do
will move mountains
so don't you dare tell me
you can't change the world

-you already have

the good the bad & the ugly

tell that person
you know who
exactly what they mean to you
because life is about being uncomfortable
and good has never come out of easy
your life will be filled with uncertainty
what you wanna do and who you wanna be
but that's precisely it
revel in the unknown and
thrive in the uncomfortable

you will beat this
not just because i believe you can
but because gravity wasn't on your side
and you just kept getting
right back up

-that is strength

if your happiness has come and gone
so will the hurt

sometimes i
can't help finding myself a little crushed
by the weight of the world
but i refuse to be squashed

-take heart

i once thought
i was not strong enough to fight this
but if i was brought to it
i will be seen through it
so here i am
fighting the good fight

the good the bad & the ugly

your darkest thoughts
try as you might
are not rooted in the truth

-it's not real

look at me
please
i beg of you
do not ever
feel like your
sadness is a
burden
i have always loved you
so much more
than the darkness
you call home

the good the bad & the ugly

ask anyone and they'll tell you i was happy
after all
i said *good* when they asked
did my homework like i was supposed to
but when i got good at the show
the audience wanted more
and so i decided to give them more
more of the truth, because
my struggle
should be talked about
and used for good
so i told someone and
they still loved me
and that is the day i took my last bow

the good the bad & the ugly

i don't think they'll understand
she sighs
they love you
i said
of course they will

-love is patient

people care
they really do
please hold on
just a little while longer
love is coming
to fix you right up

-you are not alone

find people that remind you that
this is life
and that you never want it to
stop
and then love them
don't stop

i will never get over how
people find ways to forgive and love
all the damn time

-i love people

the good the bad & the ugly

you were the only person that stopped
as i held back tears
i was in the 6th grade
and i had failed my
pre-pre algebra test
but i want you to know
it mattered
that one tiny little thing
made all the difference

-thank you

i can see the love in your eyes
when i tell you i'm tired
and just like that
i found a new home

-kind sleepy eyes

love is bigger than
your struggle

-let it in

the good the bad & the ugly

she asked me to try my best
my best is not very good
i said
nonsense she said
it's everything good
in the world

what are you most afraid of
he whispers
not that i'm not good enough,
but i'm more than enough
i say
what's scary about that?
he asks
i am filled with power and warmth and light
what am i supposed to do

-our greatest fear is not that we are inadequate, it is that we are powerful beyond measure. it is
our light, and not our darkness that frightens us

the good the bad & the ugly

she said
i don't know what to do
i said
you can start by living
as long as
there is air in your lungs
the world keeps spinning
and magic is out there

-you just gotta look for it

you filled my soul
with wonder
and my days with
deep belly laughter
and i swear to god
when you laughed
the whole world couldn't help
but dance

the good the bad & the ugly

you don't deserve the world
you deserve the whole damn galaxy

-can't you see

you do realize
what you do from
the moment you open those
big brown eyes
is entirely important to the
health of the universe

my heart was happy when i saw
you knew your own worth
and acted like it

the good the bad & the ugly

today that glass ceiling
was shaken
but not shattered
but us nasty women
won't stop
till it's done
everyday we knock
a little harder
and more often
until it all comes tumbling
down

-i stand with her

today
my lungs are filled with oxygen and
my heart is filled with love

-and that's how it's supposed to be

today
i got my grades back
and the letters of the alphabet stared back at me
and for a second i doubted i had what it took
to change the world
but not everyone needs calculus
to do so

-grades aren't everything

the good the bad & the ugly

life is beautiful
not in a i need to post this
on my snapchat sort of way
but in a it demands your
full attention kind of way

-look up

the good the bad & the ugly

this year
hit me with so many things that had
the power to destroy me
things that i could spend all day
overthinking
but what is done is done
and i have done what's most important-
believed with all my heart that
it was gonna be okay

things didn't go my way
but it wasn't my way
in the first place

the healing found me at my
worst
and the pain turned
into rhymes and
stanzas

the good the bad & the ugly

you should never have to apologize for the love you give others
for your ability to speak gently, act kindly, love deeply
is everything

-and no one should make you doubt that

some people need more love than others
and to them we will love with all we have

i waited 17 minutes to text you back
because god forbid i seem desperate
in those 17 minutes
i watched the clock
and thought about all the reasons i loved you
and then i thought
what if i didn't wait
what if i told you
because god forbid i seem desperate
but god forbid the people that matter know they matter
so i picked up my phone
and texted you back

-text them back

the good the bad & the ugly

our brains are wired
to survive
but not to thrive
so let us seek to find the goodness
in all things

-mindfulness saved me

so i think maybe
we should not strive for
happiness
but instead for joy
in little moments and
good people to share them with

think of all the things you do that give you absolutely
no pleasure
now think of the ones that do

-easy as that

the good the bad & the ugly

speak to yourself
the way you would
to an old friend

it is a standard of grace
not perfection
that we should hold ourselves to

there are many things you cannot control
for example
what they think and how they feel
to worry would be a waste of
precious time and energy
you could put towards
what you can

you do not need to justify why
you need to put yourself first
right now and always

-it's a goddamn right

the bad

the good the bad & the ugly

show compassion to those
who have wronged you
show them how you love
in the good the bad
the ugly
maybe then
they will learn

the good the bad & the ugly

i don't want them to know
my life isn't perfect
i spent 17 years
building up that lie
they don't want me to know
their life isn't perfect either
they've come too far
to give up now
so here we find ourselves
in a stalemate
waiting to see who breaks
first

the good the bad & the ugly

you scream
because you missed your bus and
spilled your coffee and
stepped in a puddle and
i will remember people aren't kind
when the world isn't kind to them
and the next time you scream
i will remember you are yelling at the
bus and the coffee and the puddle
and not me

-perspective

the good the bad & the ugly

it's days like these
i miss clean sheets and
singing at the top of my lungs
how easy it was
how good it was
how hard it is
how good it's gonna
be

-homesickness

the good the bad & the ugly

she is either on top of
or under the world
and that is okay
she does not wrestle with
the right or wrong
of it all
she's mastered how to
just be

i told her i was sad
and she whispered *me too*
and in that moment
i have never felt more connected
to the human race

the good the bad & the ugly

you must walk away if he
is your better half
you are too far too whole to
settle
for a fraction of what you
are

i was the wildest of flowers
in a field full of weeds
but he liked
roses

you mean the world to me
but there are other planets
you know

-walking away

the good the bad & the ugly

but why bother
why try
if people only disappoint
because we never know
whose heart is hurting a little extra today
and if they could
use just a little more love

-so we have to at least try

the good the bad & the ugly

people suck
but they don't always mean to
you must understand
they don't always mean to

the way people treat you is not a reflection of who you are

-i can't say that enough

since when did i start caring what other people thought
and stop thinking about how i could love them

the good the bad & the ugly

your idea of selfish is
beginning to love yourself
the way you love others

the good the bad & the ugly

i've never minded sharing
so i put my happiness in other people
and other things and
found thorns in places
that thorns weren't
supposed to be
so i took them out
and learned to be
whole on my own

please do not grow weeds
out of the dirt that has been given to you

the ugly

the good the bad & the ugly

and on that day
that road stretched out ahead of you
for what seemed like forever
and you screamed your favorite song
and thought what a wonderful life it was
and all i can think about now is
how you deserved to live it

that could've been me
why not me
and when i had cried every tear out of my body
i rose
and hugged the people i loved a little tighter
and vowed to do some good in this world

-survivor's guilt

the good the bad & the ugly

when she cannot get out of bed
and does not see the point in
eating or sleeping now that
he is gone
tell her she is not alone in this world
you must
ask her if she wants to talk and
take her out to breakfast and
hold her until she falls asleep and
tell her she makes you so proud and
repeat

-how to fix a broken heart

the good the bad & the ugly

you told me you'd been sad for a very long time
so i promised myself i'd always speak softly
and show you how to love the little things
but the sadness took away
all the little things and
just like that
i forgot how to speak softly

-*sorry*

the good the bad & the ugly

i was in such a place that
i thought if i tripped
i would never be able to
get back up again
to think that a shoelace
could break me

-not anymore

it was so dark
and i was so alone
i found me
cause that's all that was left

-the wilderness

the sadness knocked
the air out of my lungs
and brought me to my knees
i stayed there for forever

-2 days

the stars have a way of making me feel
really small
but you
you made me feel even smaller

the good the bad & the ugly

do not make someone feel less
for writing poetry
on a friday night
much like you
should not make someone feel less
for drinking themselves sick
on a friday night

-it's called coping

Printed in Great Britain
by Amazon